FRIENDSHIP

ISSUE

ideals

The fairest flower in the garden
of life
Is the fellowship of friends;
Time but glorifies its beauty
With a fragrance that never ends.

No cloud can shade its loveliness,
No storm its petals part,
For the flower of friendship
dwells forever
In the shrine of the human heart.

editor
Maryjane Hooper Tonn

•

managing editor
Lorraine Obst

•

assistant managing editor
Ralph Luedtke

•

associate editor
Charles Roberts

IDEALS—Vol. 32, No. 1—January, MCMLXXV. Published bimonthly by IDEALS PUBLISHING CORP., 11315 Watertown Plank Road,
Milwaukee, Wis. 53226. Second-class postage paid at Milwaukee, Wisconsin. Copyright © MCMLXXIV by IDEALS PUBLISHING CORP.
All rights reserved. Title IDEALS registered U.S. Patent Office.
ONE YEAR SUBSCRIPTION—six consecutive issues as published—only $8.50
TWO YEAR SUBSCRIPTION—twelve consecutive issues as published—only $16.00
SINGLE ISSUES—only $2.25

Begin the Day With Friendliness

Begin the day with friendliness
   And only friends you'll find.
Yes, greet the dawn with happiness;
   Keep happy thoughts in mind.
Salute the day with peaceful thoughts,
   And peace will fill your heart;
Begin the day with joyful soul,
   And joy will be your part.

Begin the day with friendliness,
   Keep friendly all day long,
Keep in your soul a friendly thought,
   Your heart a friendly song.
Have in your mind a word of cheer
   For all who come your way,
And they will bless you too, in turn,
   And wish you "Happy day!"

Begin each day with friendly thoughts,
   And as the day goes on,
Keep friendly, loving, good and kind,
   Just as you were at dawn.
The day will be a friendly one,
   And then at night you'll find
That you were happy all day long
   Through friendly thoughts in mind.

Frank B. Whitney

Photograph opposite:
A. Devaney, Inc.

I Wish You

Friend of mine, in the year oncoming
I wish you a little time for play,
And an hour to dream in the eerie gloaming
After the clamorous day.
(And the moon like a pearl from an Indian shore
To hang for a lantern above your door.)

A little house with friendly rafters,
And someone in it to need you there,
Wine of romance and wholesome laughters
With a comrade or two to share.
(And some secret spot of your very own
Whenever you want to cry alone.)

I wish you a garden on fire with roses,
Columbines planted for your delight,
Scent of mint in its shadowy closes,
Clean, gay winds at night.
(Some nights for sleeping and some to ride
With the broomstick witches far and wide.)

A goodly crop of figs to gather,
With a thistle or two to prick and sting;
Since a harvesting too harmless is rather
An unadventurous thing.
(And now and then, spite of reason or rule,
The chance to be a bit of a fool.)

I wish you a thirst that can never be sated
For all the loveliness earth can yield,
Slim, cool birches whitely mated,
Dawn on an April field.
(And never too big a bill to pay
When the fiddler finds he must up and away.)

L. M. Montgomery

People

We do not live in houses, but in heartbeats
Of people who share every day with us.
We grow rich in companionship.
The heart meets and greets its own
    and life is glorious.

Anne Campbell

Friendship

Casual friendships come and go much as the
currents ebb and flow. The swells and ripples
that they make leave mixed emotions in their
wake. For some friends drift with changing
tide. They come on strong and then subside,
only to crash upon the shore, disappear and
be seen no more!

Others are strong enough to stand the
changing tides and shifting sand. And what
sets these friendships apart? Affinity of mind
and heart, love much more than just a
token, thoughts understood yet unspoken,
a common bond, a mutual goal, an
understanding heart and soul, a hand
outstretched in time of need, a thoughtful
and a friendly deed.

These little things that mean so much are
strokes of friendship's velvet touch!

Donita M. Dyer

Photograph opposite
SANDSTONE ARCH
Natural Bridges State Park,
Santa Cruz, California
Photo – Alpha

from

the editor's

scrapbook

A friend is a present you give yourself.

Robert Louis Stevenson

Blessed are the peacemakers: for they shall be called the children of God.

Matthew 5:9

A friend is a person with whom I may think aloud . . . A friend may well be reckoned the masterpiece of nature . . . I do then with my friends as I do with my books, I would have them where I can find them, but I seldom use them . . . Happy is the house that shelters a friend.

Ralph Waldo Emerson

You can take your troubles to others, but you can't leave them there.

Translated from the African Hausas Tribe

It is easy to say how we love new friends, and what we think of them, but words can never trace out all the fibres that knit us to the old.

George Eliot

Friendship is the triple alliance of the three great powers: love, sympathy and help.

Author Unknown

I pray thee, O God, that I may be beautiful within.

Socrates

This my commandment, That ye love one another, as I have loved you. Greater love hath no man than this, that a man lay down his life for his friends.

John 15:12-13

An old friend is like a full-blown rose, each velvet petal a pleasant memory. Its fragrance recalls sweetness that grows with years of love, understanding and sympathy.

Margaret Crawford

Keep making new friends as you travel through life — so you won't be left alone.

Martin Vanbee

Friendship is a plant of slow growth, and must undergo and withstand the shocks of adversity before it is entitled to the appellation.

George Washington

There are quiet hours and lonely hours,
And hours that have no end;
But the wonderful hour is the evening hour,
When you walk beside a friend.

Author Unknown

Happiness is best attained by learning to live each day by itself. The worries are mostly about yesterday and tomorrow.

Michael Nolan

A friendship true is like pure gold —
It won't wear out because it's old.

Harriett Meisenheimer

There are two things that go into the makeup of friendship, the one is truth, the other is understanding.

Author Unknown

Friendship makes prosperity brighter, while it lightens adversity by sharing its griefs and anxieties.

Cicero

May the road rise up to meet you,
May the wind be always at your back,
May the sun shine warm upon your face,
And rains fall soft upon your fields.
And until we meet again,
May God hold you in the palm of His hand.

An Old Irish Blessing

PENN'S TREATY WITH THE INDIANS
At Shackamaxon (now Kensington) in 1682
Benjamin West

In recognition of the forthcoming Bicentennial of the United States, Ideals pays tribute to the American past with these pages on William Penn and Benjamin Franklin.

Quaker Friendship

This is the Comfort of Friends, that though they may be said to Die, yet their Friendship and Society are, in the best Sense, ever present, because immortal.

Friendship is the next Pleasure we may hope for: and where we find it not at Home, or have no home to find it in, we may seek it abroad. It is an Union of Spirits, a Marriage of Hearts, and the Bond thereto Vertue.

There can be no Friendship where there is no Freedom. Friendship loves a Free Air, and will not be penned up in straight and narrow Enclosures. It will speak freely, and act so too; and take nothing ill where no ill is meant; nay, where it is, 'twill easily Forgive, and forget too, upon small Acknowledgments.

Friends are true Twins in soul; they sympathize in every thing, and have the same Love and Aversion.

One is not happy without the other, nor can either of them be miserable alone: as if they take their turns in Pain as well as in Pleasure; relieving one another in their most adverse Conditions.

What one enjoys the other cannot Want. Like the Primitive Christians, they have all things in common, no Property but in one another.

A true Friend unbosoms freely, advises justly, assists readily, adventures boldly, takes all patiently, defends courageously.

These being the Qualities of a Friend, we are to find them before we choose one.

William Penn

Elfreth's Alley: Since 1690 the oldest continuously inhabited street in the United States.

Benjamin Franklin and Philadelphia

**From his "Autobiography,"
Benjamin Franklin
describes his first acquaintance
with the "City of Brotherly Love"
as a young man of twenty.**

I have been the more particular in this description of my journey, and shall be so of my first entry into that city, that you may in your mind compare such unlikely beginnings with the figure I have since made there. I was in my working dress, my best cloaths being to come round by sea. I was dirty from my journey; my pockets were stuff'd out with shirts and stockings, and I knew no soul nor where to look for lodging. I was fatigued with travelling, rowing and want of rest, I was very hungry; and my whole stock of cash consisted of a Dutch dollar, and about a shilling in copper. The latter I gave the people of the boat for my passage, who at first refus'd it, on account of my rowing; but I insisted on their taking it. A man being sometimes more generous when he has but a little money than when he has plenty, perhaps thro' fear of being thought to have but little.

Then I walked up the street, gazing about till near the market-house I met a boy with bread. I had made many a meal on bread, and, inquiring where he got it, I went immediately to the baker's he directed me to, in Second-street, and ask'd for bisket, intending such as we had in Boston; but they, it seems, were not made in Philadelphia. Then I asked for a three-penny loaf, and was told they had none such. So not considering or knowing the difference of money, and the greater cheapness nor the names of his bread, I bad him give me three-penny worth of any sort. He gave me, accordingly, three great puffy rolls. I was surpriz'd at the quantity, but took it, and, having no room in my pockets, walk'd off with a roll under each arm, and eating the other. Thus I went up Market-street as far as Fourth-street, passing by the door of Mr. Read, my future wife's father; when she, standing at the door, saw me, and thought I made, as I certainly did, a most awkward, ridiculous appearance. Then I turned and went down Chestnut-street and part of Walnut-street, eating my roll all the way, and, coming round, found myself again at Market-street wharf, near the boat I came in, to which I

Philadelphia in 1735 about ten years after Benjamin Franklin's arrival.

went for a draught of the river water; and, being filled with one of my rolls, gave the other two to a woman and her child that came down the river in the boat with us, and were waiting to go farther.

Thus refreshed, I walked again up the street, which by this time had many clean-dressed people in it, who were all walking the same way. I joined them, and thereby was led into the great meeting-house of the Quakers near the market. I sat down among them, and, after looking round awhile and hearing nothing said, being very drowsy thro' labor and want of rest the preceding night, I fell fast asleep, and continu'd so till the meeting broke up, when one was kind enough to rouse me. This was, therefore, the first house I was in, or slept in, in Philadelphia.

Benjamin Franklin

Franklin on Friendship

Be slow in choosing a friend,
slower in changing.

Thou can'st not joke an enemy into a friend,
but thou may'st a friend into an enemy.

When befriended, remember it:
When you befriend, forget it.

Friendship increases by visiting friends,
but by visiting seldom.

A brother may not be a friend,
but a friend will always be a brother.

Friendship cannot live with ceremony,
nor without civility.

Friends are the true scepters of princes.

If you would be loved, love and be lovable.

Friends

You ask me why I like him. Nay,
I cannot; nay, I would not, say.
I think it vile to pigeonhole
The pros and cons of a kindred soul.

You wonder he should be my friend.
But then why should you comprehend,
Thank God for this . . . a new . . . surprise:
My eyes, remember, are not your eyes.

Cherish this one small mystery,
And marvel not that love can be
In spite of all his many flaws.
In spite? Supposing I said, "Because."

A truce, a truce to questioning:
"We two are friends" tells everything.
Yet if you must know, this is why:
Because he is he and I am I.

Edward Verrall Lucas

KINDRED SPIRITS

Asher B. Durand
American, 1796-1886

My Dearest Friend

We hope that you enjoy our latest addition to Ideals, *a Harlequin short story, complete on five pages.*

Lesley Wilson

Jackie had never expected, when she came to London to share a flat with her cousin Mary, to find herself waiting with such eagerness for the first sight of her old friend Pete.

It was evening and the shops over which she and Mary lived were dark and silent, but from the main road she could hear the roar of the traffic, and the sound of people laughing, talking as they hurried along.

Jackie sighed a little. She had known Pete all her life. She had toddled trustingly after him as a small child, and as they grew up, Pete had always been around to take her to a dance, or make up a four at tennis. Nothing would please their parents more, they both knew, than if they managed to fall in love. But that was a joke Jackie and Pete shared between them, and although she had missed Pete when he had left for London two years ago, it was only to please her mother that she had promised to get in touch with him.

At first, London had seemed so new and exciting. The bustle and the shops and the people; the traffic and the noise. The little flat was like a palace; cooking in the tiny kitchen was fun and Mary's friends were delightful. But after a while, a disturbing loneliness began to haunt Jackie. Mary's friends were Mary's friends — most of the young men already had a girl in tow. The busy streets and crowded cafes seemed alien and resentful when she was in them alone; and although the job she'd found was well paid, it was in a solicitor's office where even the junior clerk was well over forty.

So, on an impulse, unable to bear the thought of another lonely evening, she had telephoned Pete. Now, from her window, she saw his lanky figure pass under a street lamp, and she turned from the window to glance quickly into a mirror which hung on the wall. The action surprised her and she grinned suddenly. She had never worried how she looked, for Pete. All the same, it would be nice to see him again, hear his familiar voice and feel comfortable and at ease with an old friend.

Pete, had she known it, was climbing the stairs to the flat in some trepidation. He had known Jackie was in London, and had been telling himself he ought to do something about it. He was fond of her — she was a grand kid. All the same, his life was very full and busy and Jackie was part of a rather dull past which he had left behind.

When she opened the door and flung her arms round him, just as she used to when she came home from boarding school, he found he'd forgotten how very small and slight she was, and how her skin, still tanned from the summer sun, glowed with health.

"Pete . . . How nice," she was saying.

He rumpled her hair a little awkwardly, before he stepped back out of her arms. "Nice to see you, Jackie."

She coloured a little, as if she had been surprised by his withdrawal, and led the way into the sitting room. Mary, who knew Pete from spending holidays with Jackie's parents, was just about to go out, and had time to say no more than hello and good-bye. Then the door slammed and they were left alone, an odd silence growing between them.

They broke it together: "What would you like . . . ?"

"How have you been . . . ?"

They laughed, and all at once they were back on the old familiar footing again with Pete, as usual, giving the orders: "Go and get your coat on. We'll go out for a meal. There's a place just round the corner that's quite good."

* * *

The crowded, noisy roads seemed friendly and amusing now that Pete was at her side, and the music that blared from transistors made her want to dance. Pete took her to a small, dark restaurant where the tables were close together, and young people perched on stools at a sandwich bar, waving their arms and talking. Jackie looked round, her eyes sparkling, and loved it all.

During the soup, she brought him up to date on all their old friends at home. While they ate fried chicken she told him about her job, and how dull it was. "Mary's friend Michael thinks he can get me a job in his firm. His boss's assistant wants a secretary. Michael thinks I might do." She didn't add, for some reason, that Mary had said the boss's assistant in question was "quite a dish."

Pete poured her some more tea. "I'm sure you'll do. Good secretaries aren't all that easy to come by — especially if they're attractive," he added, matter-of-factly. "So many of the prettier girls seem to work in boutiques or are models, or something — like Amanda." His eyes softened and

Continued

*Photograph opposite:
Jack Zehrt*

took on a dreamy, faraway look which Jackie was to know only too well, in the weeks to come.

Amanda, he told her, was beautiful. She was tall and slim, with eyelashes an inch long, and every time he met her, her hair was a different colour.

"Doesn't it make it rather difficult to recognise her?" Jackie asked innocently.

Pete stopped in full flood and gave her a hard look. "You'd recognise Amanda in sack cloth and ashes. There's something about her."

Jackie asked Mary about Amanda.

Her cousin made a face; "Amanda has the face of an angel, a voice like honey and a soul of pure vitriol."

Jackie was startled. "Pete says she's such a gentle, unaffected girl. Do you think he'll marry her?"

"I don't think she'll marry Pete," Mary corrected. "She's out for bigger fish. But make no mistake, she won't let him slip out of her net until she's good and ready. Pete makes a nice background. He's good looking and has nice manners. He does her very well as an escort."

"Yes. I suppose so," Jackie said unhappily. She hoped Pete wasn't going to get hurt.

Michael's boss's assistant, whom Jackie saw the next day, was "a dish." He had dark, wavy hair and blue eyes that crinkled at the corners when he smiled.

Jackie got the job, and bought a new suit on the way home — for the sake of the job, of course.

It was ten days before the girls saw Pete again. Mary was dressing to go out and Jackie, who was experimenting with a new hairdo, was in rollers. Pete was ruffled and cold and somehow rather forlorn, so Jackie asked him to stay to supper, and they fried bacon and eggs and ate cheese and apples. She told him about her new job.

"Jason's terribly nice, he —"

"Jason? Nobody can be called Jason!"

"Well, he is," she said defiantly. "And he doesn't like to be called Mr. Cooper."

Pete's eyebrows drew down sharply over his eyes. "How old is he?"

"Oh, thirty-ish," Jackie said airily. "I'm told they think a lot of him in the firm. It must be a very good job. He's got a flat in town, and his family live in the country . . ."

"Family?"

"Mmm." Jackie poured more coffee. "Parents, I suppose. How's Amanda?" she added.

Pete, it turned out, had had a date with Amanda that evening, but she had cancelled it. She had the chance to meet a big advertising agent at a party. "He's just got a contract for some telly ads," Pete explained. "If he thinks she's the right girl for them, it'll be her first big break. She'll get it, of course," he added. "She's wonderful. You must meet her."

★   ★   ★

Jackie met her about a week later, at a party. She looked Jackie up and down. "So you're the old friend. I've heard all about you," she said sweetly. "We must lunch one day — or something." As she led Pete away with one hand on his arm, Jackie heard her bell-like tones: "What a sweet person. And how right you are! Exactly the girl-next-door type."

Jackie glowered at her tousle-headed reflection when she got home, wondering if it made her look older or younger. But Jason liked it. They'd drifted into the habit of having lunch together now and then, or a drink after they'd finished at the office. His blue eyes crinkled at her, and his warm tones turned her bones to water.

One evening he asked Jackie if she could stay and finish a report. "We'll go back to the flat — it'll be more comfortable," he said.

Jackie's well disciplined instincts rang every kind of warning bell, but she told herself she was being unsophisticated, and allowed him to buy her dinner on the way.

The flat was small and elegant. There were a lot of photographs of a young woman and two children.

"My wife and the kids," he said casually, pouring some drinks. "We're getting a divorce." Then, seeing her wooden face, he smiled. "Don't tell me you didn't know?"

"No. I thought —"

"It doesn't make any difference, does it?" he asked, his voice sinking to velvety depths. "Not to us . . .?" and he reached out his arms for her.

Jackie fought her way free and escaped. The whole thing was very undignified and left her burning with shame. He called her several very rude names and said she'd been leading him on. She got herself a taxi after waiting for ages and cried all the way home.

The next day she gave in her notice and worked her week out in stony silence. Pete, demanding to know why she'd left, got the story out of her. To Jackie's astonishment he looked so angry that she grew quite frightened. He even seemed to blame himself.

"I should have guessed. I should have warned you. Office wolves — they're all over the place. I'd like to go and kick his false teeth in."

In spite of herself, Jackie giggled. "They are not false."

"I bet you they are. And I'll bet he wears a toupee as well," he snorted.

Suddenly Jackie, who hadn't been quite sure if she was suffering a broken heart, decided she wasn't.

"And talking of hair," Pete added, "I don't like yours like that."

"I don't either," Jackie agreed.

She washed it when he'd gone and the next day she went and got herself another job with the buyer of the stationery department of a large store. Mr. Jones, the buyer, was elderly and gentle and his whole interest lay in typewriters and paper, letter headings and envelopes. The staff rooms were pleasant, the canteen excellent, and there was a large young man called Robert from the sports department, who took one look at Jackie, and carried his plate to her table at lunch the next day.

The glamorous Amanda became engaged to the advertising agent. Pete came round wearing an anguished expression. "Sometimes I thought she and I — but I suppose she was just using me."

"Shows what an idiot she is," Jackie snorted. "Honestly, Pete, she really was incredibly stupid. She never talked of anything but herself, and she worried so about her looks. I bet she never went out in the car with you, with the hood down?"

"Well, no . . ."

"Did you ever go swimming with her? Most of that gorgeous hair was false."

"I suppose you'd know."

"And it must take her hours to go to bed at night. Mary's bad enough," she added, throwing her cousin to the wolves without compunction, "but Amanda — by the time she's taken off everything she's stuck on, I don't know what would be left."

Pete considered, and grinned. "It could give one quite a shock, I suppose." He stood up and held out his hand. "Let's go and find somewhere to dance."

★   ★   ★

Robert was a sporty type. Jackie spent Saturday afternoons muffled to the eyebrows on wet fields watching him rushing around in the mud with lots of other healthy young men, and Saturday evenings listening to them all going over the finer points of the game.

Continued

And Pete met Claudine.

Claudine was dark and sombre and artistic. She felt everything very deeply, Pete told Jackie. When Jackie met her, Claudine looked her up and down as Amanda had, and Jackie heard her telling Pete, "She has good bones, but there's no suffering in her face."

"There should be," Jackie thought, as she snuffled through her third cold in quick succession. She was relieved to give up Robert for David in the music department.

David took her to concerts and the ballet. They always walked home afterwards because he said they had to reorientate themselves after such an experience. He never seemed to think that Jackie might want to eat, so Jackie, who had a healthy appetite, took to asking him back to the flat and cooking him supper, while they listened to his latest records.

Mary complained about the depleted store cupboard. "He doesn't want a girl — he wants a meal ticket."

Pete couldn't stand David. "What on earth can you see in that wet week?"

"He's not wet. Just because he happens to prefer classical music to your kind of rubbish."

"What do you mean, my kind of rubbish? I happen to like concerts and ballet, too."

"I've never known you to go to any."

"You don't know everything. Besides, I know his type. You've only to look at him to see what he's after."

"And what is he after?" Jackie said dangerously.

"Well . . ." Pete went red and fell silent, and when Mary came in, he mumbled some excuse and left.

What David was after, in fact, was a girl who could afford better seats for the ballet, and he found one, so Jackie saw him no more.

* * *

Pete had been sent out of town by his firm, when Jackie met Hugh. He was down from the North. He took one look at Jackie, liked what he saw, and set about acquiring her in much the same way as his father would have set about buying another mill or another valuable piece of property. In the days that followed Hugh telephoned her regularly, drove her home from work, took her out to lunch during the week and driving in the country at the weekends.

By the time Pete got back, Hugh was a habit. They ran into Pete with his new girl friend one evening at the theatre, during the interval. Gale was blonde, clinging and very spoilt, and she was also very possessive towards Pete, which irritated Jackie enormously.

On the way home from the theatre Hugh asked Jackie to marry him. Panic seized her, and while she stammered over some kind of reply, he said reasonably, "But why not, Jackie? I'd make you a good husband. I can give you everything you want. I think we're very well suited. You must come up North and meet my parents. There's even a house there I've had my eye on for some time. If you liked it, I would buy it."

"How — how nice," Jackie said inanely. "And you must come and meet mine — my parents, I mean."

Hugh put his hand over hers in the darkness of the taxi. "I'll be glad to. I'll need to speak to your father, won't I?" he added, as if, Jackie thought wildly, she'd already accepted him.

* * *

"He's a stuffed shirt," Pete stormed at her when she told him of Hugh's proposal. "You can't marry him. He's old, he's staid."

Jackie flared up at him. "You don't think any of my friends are right. Hugh is kind and generous and reliable."

"You sound as if you're employing a nanny or buying a horse. This is a man we're talking about."

"Hugh *is* a man."

"A man who'll marry you and buy you a house and furnish it. Who'll go out after breakfast and come home at night, and never even stop to find out if you're happy. Has he ever said he loved you?"

Jackie turned away quickly. "Hugh doesn't go in much for flowery speeches."

"Has he ever asked you if you love him?" Pete reached for Jackie's shoulder and turned her to face him. "Come to that, do you love him?"

Jackie hesitated, "I wouldn't think of marrying him if I didn't," she said truthfully.

Pete pushed his hand through his hair so that it stood up as it had done when he was a boy. "Well, let me know the date, won't you? I'll dance at your wedding."

Jackie asked Hugh for time to think, and when he gave it a little impatiently, wondered why she felt so depressed when she ought to be feeling so happy. If she were honest with herself, hadn't her main reason for coming to London been to get married — eventually? But did she want it just yet? And with Hugh?

"You could do a lot worse," Mary said candidly, and added, "How's Pete?"

"I don't know," Jackie said crossly. "Ask Gale."

* * *

When Jackie got home from work one Monday night, the telephone was ringing. It was Brian Heywood, a young journalist who had the flat below Pete's.

He sounded apologetic: "I'm sorry to bother you, but I don't know who else to get on to. I've got to go away for my paper, you see, on the night train, and he's got a raging temperature. But he won't have the doctor and I know you're old friends and —"

"What are you talking about?" Jackie asked firmly.

"Pete — I think he's got flu."

Jackie hesitated. Hugh had had to attend a business dinner that evening and would probably be too tied up to telephone. "I'll come round," she said.

Brian was vastly relieved to see her. "Pete didn't want me to ring, but I couldn't go away and just leave him lying there."

"What about Gale?"

"Who? Oh, she wouldn't be much good. Anyway, I don't think he sees her now."

Pete lay in a huddle of bedclothes, flushed and with over-bright eyes. Jackie felt his head and asked Brian to telephone for the doctor. When the doctor arrived, he scowled and asked how long Pete had been like this.

"He's been getting worse all weekend. I've been doing my best, but . . ."

"Should have sent for me sooner. Now . . ." the doctor pulled out his prescription pad and began to write. "Can someone go to the chemist's?"

"I've time, before my train goes," Brian offered and left for the chemist's while Jackie went back to Pete, who had fallen into a restless sleep.

Once he opened his eyes and smiled at her. "Jackie . . ." he murmured but, before she could do more than put her hand over his, he had drifted away again.

"What are we going to do?" Brian asked anxiously. "We can't just leave him here. There is a woman who comes in to clean, but she's not due until tomorrow, and anyway I don't know her address."

"I'll stay," Jackie said.

She rang Mary at the flat. Her cousin sounded concerned for Pete, then faintly amused. "What do I tell Hugh if he should ring?"

"He won't. He told me to go to bed early."

"And of course, he'd never think you'd dare to disobey!"

Jackie slept on the sofa in the sitting room, Pete's coats piled on top of her. In the morning, he was not much better. He didn't even seem surprised to see her when she brought him tea, and straightened his bedclothes. He obviously could not be left, so she telephoned Mr. Jones at the store and said she wouldn't be in. "My friend has flu," she said, evasively.

Mr. Jones was more understanding. "It's nice to hear of young people being so unselfish. Flu can be very nasty. I hope your friend will be better soon."

"Yes, yes . . . thank you. I mean, I hope so too."

Later, the doctor came and he took Pete's temperature. He scowled at Jackie. "You his sister?"

"No. But I'm an old friend. I've known him ever since I was born."

The doctor grunted and smiled suddenly. "Don't worry. He'll be all right. But he needs someone here today to give him pills and so on. He'll be over the worst, soon."

Jackie looked through to the bedroom where Pete lay covered with beads of sweat and with stubble on his chin. "I can stay," she said.

*   *   *

Hugh was less understanding. Mary telephoned in a panic that evening, shortly before Hugh rang the doorbell. "I had to give him the address, Jackie. Terribly sorry."

Hugh came in, looking large and possessive. "You stayed here alone?" he asked, after she had explained.

"Well, of course I stayed alone." Jackie looked at Hugh in surprise. "I couldn't leave him as sick as he is."

"You could have got a nurse, surely?"

"I don't know if Pete can afford a nurse, and I wouldn't know how to set about getting one. Anyway, it'll only be another few days."

"Days? You don't intend to go on staying here?"

In the bedroom, Pete groaned and murmured. "Of course I intend to," she said. "My mother, and Pete's, would never forgive me if I didn't."

"And I will find it hard to forgive you if you do. Jackie, I cannot allow you to spend another night here. What will people think? As my fiancée— "

"I am not your fiancée. And I don't care what other people think."

"Jackie, I insist you find someone else to look after Pete, and return to your own flat . . ."

From the bedroom a voice called faintly, "Jackie . . . Jackie . . ."

Jackie half-turned, longing to go to Pete. "No," she said. "I'm sorry, Hugh."

Hugh looked at her for a moment and then, unexpectedly, his expression softened. "I guessed you didn't love me, Jackie, though I hoped you might, one day. But why did you never tell me you loved Pete?" He patted her shoulder clumsily, turned and walked out of the room.

Jackie stood and stared at the closed door, then she went back to Pete. She sat down by his bed and looked at him. His eyelashes, she noticed for the first time, were very long. And his mouth, relaxed and tired, was sweet. He had a three day stubble on his chin and it was ginger. His hair was copper-bronze. "We will probably have redheaded children," she thought absently.

She leant forward, peering into the familiar face which suddenly seemed unfamiliar. Love him? Yes, of course she did.

Pete's eyes opened. He looked at her and she saw that all signs of his fever had gone. "Yes," he said. "Why didn't you tell anyone that you loved me?"

Jackie sat back, her face going scarlet. "You were listening."

"Yes," Pete agreed cheerfully. He put out his hand and caught hers and his eyes were firm and demanding. "And do you, Jackie? Do you love me?"

"All those girls," she said accusingly.

"All those young men," he countered. "What were we both looking for, Jackie? Only each other. And we couldn't see it."

He reached up an arm and pulled her close, turning her face away from his prickly chin and burying his own in the sweet softness of her hair. "Only each other, my dearest friend," he repeated softly.

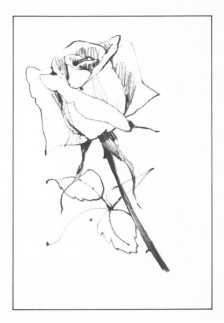

Willow Pattern

The while we sip our jasmine tea,
we learn, and not without a pang,
how once the beautiful Koong-see
was loved by poor and lowly Chang,

her father's scribe. The Mandarin
with other plans for her instead,
had pledged her to the rich Ta-jin.
Love laughs at locksmiths, it is said . . .

Across the humpbacked bridge they fly,
pursued by father threatening death!
A thousand years or more go by
and still they hasten, out of breath.

Koong-see casts one long look behind
at house, pagoda-roofed, and willow,
her childhood's home. Now they must find
in some far land a nest, a pillow . . .

The fierce Ta-jin, grown wild and rash,
curses the pair with dreadful words,
follows and burns their house to ash.
But wait—the two escape as birds!

The lovers' fate—what can it matter—
their lives and their ensuing lot?
On cup and saucer, plate and platter,
still thrives the charming, foolish plot,
the storyteller long forgot.

Amanda Benjamin Hall

THE STORY OF THE WILLOW PATTERN

The willow pattern, in the characteristic blue, has been one of the most popular designs of English pottery since the late eighteenth century. On this page is a reproduction of the original design executed by Thomas Minton about 1780 to illustrate the story of two Chinese lovers, Koong-see and Chang. Koong-see was the daughter of a wealthy mandarin. She loved her father's secretary, Chang, and he in turn, loved her. In the design we see the terrace and the summerhouse where the mandarin imprisoned his daughter. He wanted her to be the wife of the wealthy Ta-jin. From this prison Koong-see watched the willow tree blossom and wrote verses expressing her longing for Chang. Also in the design is the barricade the father erected to keep Chang away. Chang, however, rescued Koong-see and they fled over the humpbacked bridge. Her father pursued the couple, brandishing a whip. Beyond the bridge is a boat in which the lovers successfully escaped to the island in the background. There they lived happily until the rejected suitor, Ta-jin, discovered them and burned their house to the ground. The spirits of the two lovers arose from the ashes in the form of white doves to fly forever over the scene of their earthly happiness.

 # I Love You

I love you,
Not only for what you are,
But for what I am
When I am with you.

I love you,
Not only for what
You have made of yourself,
But for what
You are making of me.

I love you
For the part of me
That you bring out;
I love you
For putting your hand
Into my heaped-up heart
And passing over
All the foolish, weak things
That you can't help
Dimly seeing there,
And for drawing out
Into the light
All the beautiful belongings
That no one else had looked
Quite far enough to find.

I love you because you
Are helping me to make
Of the lumber of my life
Not a tavern
But a temple;
Out of the works
Of my every day
Not a reproach
But a song.

I love you
Because you have done
More than any creed
Could have done
To make me good,
And more than any fate
Could have done
To make me happy.

You have done it
Without a touch,
Without a word,
Without a sign.
You have done it
By being yourself,
Perhaps that is what
Being a friend means,
After all.

Author Unknown

Beautiful Things

Beautiful faces are those that wear . . .
It matters little if dark or fair . . .
Whole-souled honesty printed there.

Beautiful eyes are those that show,
Like crystal panes where hearth fires glow,
Beautiful thoughts that burn below.

Beautiful lips are those whose words
Leap from the heart like songs of birds,
Yet whose utterance prudence girds.

Beautiful hands are those that do
Work that is earnest, brave and true,
Moment by moment the long day through.

Beautiful feet are those that go
On kindly errands to and fro . . .
Down humblest ways, if God wills it so.

Beautiful lives are those that bless
Silent rivers of happiness,
Whose hidden fountains but few may guess.

Ellen Palmer Allerton

Photograph opposite
CAROUSEL HORSE
Courtesy of Cybis Porcelains
Trenton, New Jersey

Helen Keller and her teacher, Anne Sullivan

How I Learned the Meaning of Love

Helen Keller

I remember the morning that I first asked the meaning of the word, "love." This was before I knew many words. I had found a few early violets in the garden and brought them to my teacher. She tried to kiss me; but at that time I did not like to have anyone kiss me except my mother. Miss Sullivan put her arm gently around me and spelled into my hand, "I love Helen."

"What is love?" I asked.

She drew me closer to her and said, "It is here," pointing to my heart, whose beats I was conscious of for the first time. Her words puzzled me very much because I did not then understand anything unless I touched it.

I smelt the violets in her hand and asked, half in words, half in signs, a question which meant, "Is love the sweetness of flowers?"

"No," said my teacher.

Again I thought. The warm sun was shining on us.

"Is this not love?" I asked, pointing in the direction from which the heat came. "Is this not love?"

It seemed to me that there could be nothing more beautiful than the sun, whose warmth makes all things grow. But Miss Sullivan shook her head, and I was greatly puzzled and disappointed. I thought it strange that my teacher could not show me love.

A day or two afterward I was stringing beads of different sizes in symmetrical groups . . . two large beads, three small ones, and so on. I had made many mistakes, and Miss Sullivan had pointed them out again and again with gentle patience. Finally I noticed a very obvious error in the sequence and for an instant I concentrated my attention on the lesson and tried to think how I should have arranged the beads. Miss Sullivan touched my forehead and spelled with decided emphasis, "Think."

In a flash I knew that the word was the name of the process that was going on in my head. This was my first conscious perception of an abstract idea.

For a long time I was still . . . I was not thinking of the beads in my lap, but trying to find a meaning for "love" in the light of this new idea. The sun had been under a cloud all day, and there had been brief showers; but suddenly the sun broke forth in all its southern splendor.

Again I asked my teacher, "Is this not love?"

"Love is something like the clouds that were in the sky before the sun came out," she replied. Then in simpler words than these, which at that time I could not have understood, she explained: "You cannot touch the clouds, you know, but you feel the rain and know how glad the flowers and thirsty earth are to have it after a hot day. You cannot touch love either; but you feel the sweetness that it pours into everything. Without love you would not be happy or want to play."

The beautiful truth burst open my mind . . . I felt that there were invisible lines stretched between my spirit and the spirits of others.

Ivy Green, the birthplace of Helen Keller in Tuscumbia, Alabama

A Valentine

Once a year we turn our thoughts to a valentine,
A dainty card of lace and verse where dreams and love entwine.
'Tis like a lovely sweet refrain singing in each heart;
We choose our valentine with care to play its special part.
Sometimes it's made with little hands and, oh, the effort there!
Though full of paste and crooked print, it's beautiful and fair.
Sometimes it may be purchased and selected carefully
To send upon its merry way for our loved ones to see.
Each valentine has magic and contains three priceless things . . .
Love and joy and memories that caring always brings.

LaVerne P. Larson

Daily Valentines

How sweet to get a valentine
Of plain or fancy art,
A rose so pink and violets, too,
Or satin-covered heart.

But more than beauty or design,
We prize the words that say
The sender's love comes with the gift
In quite the warmest way.

We like to know that someone cares,
That someone wants to do
The kindly deed that makes us feel
Well loved and happy, too.

So why not give expression then,
To love for friends so dear,
Not only on one certain day
But many times a year?

Our valentines may be a smile,
A cheerful word or two,
A helping hand, a tender glance
That signals, "I love you."

And if we often take the time
To give these friendly signs,
The world will soon be brightened by
Our daily valentines.

Cleo King

The Month of Valentines

February is the month of cold and
   ice and snow,
The month when winter rules supreme
   and blustery winds do blow,
When grown-up folks are quite content
   to sit beside the fire,
To pop some corn or read a book,
   their favorite heart's desire.

February is the month when sledding
   is such fun,
When skiing is the favorite sport
   of almost everyone;
The precious month of joys complete
   and pleasant happy times,
The month of candy, hearts and flowers,
   the month of valentines.

February is the month when sweethearts
   share a dream,
The month of winter still to be,
   the month of not quite spring;
A very dear and lovely month with
   precious dreams sublime . . .
It brings a happiness complete,
   the month of valentines.

Garnett Ann Schultz

The Snowstorm

Announced by all the trumpets of the sky,
Arrives the snow, and, driving o'er the fields,
Seems nowhere to alight: the whited air
Hides hills and woods, the river, and the heaven,
And veils the farmhouse at the garden's end.
The sled and traveller stopped, the courier's feet
Delayed, all friends shut out, the housemates sit
Around the radiant fireplace, enclosed
In a tumultuous privacy of storm.

Come see the north wind's masonry.
Out of an unseen quarry evermore
Furnished with tile, the fierce artificer
Curves his white bastions with projected roof
Round every windward stake, or tree, or door.
Speeding, the myriad-handed, his wild work
So fanciful, so savage, nought cares he
For number or proportion. Mockingly,
On coop or kennel he hangs Parian wreaths;
A swan-like form invests the hidden thorn;
Fills up the farmer's lane from wall to wall,
Maugre the farmer's sighs; and at the gate
A tapering turret overtops the work.

And when his hours are numbered, and the world
Is all his own, retiring, as he were not,
Leaves, when the sun appears, astonished Art
To mimic in slow structures, stone by stone,
Built in an age, the mad wind's night-work,
The frolic architecture of the snow.

Ralph Waldo Emerson

Childhood Friendship

Remember when we were little girls
    and I lived across from you?
Remember when both of us wore long curls
    tied back with bows of blue?

Remember the days in wintertime
    when we walked together to school;
While snowdrifts covered the streets outside,
    we recited the golden rule.

Remember the days with buggies and dolls
    when we played at keeping house,
And you wore your mother's high-heeled shoes
    while I wore Mama's blouse?

For you were my favorite, my very best friend,
    and I was your first choice, too,
And we learned of the give and take of life
    as our childhood friendship grew.

Mildred Spires Jacobs

Memory

Long ago is not so far away . . .
It's close as thought
And near as memory
Jogged by a souvenir,
Stirred by a keepsake
From days that used to be.

Long ago is not so far away . . .
For mind and memory
Span both years and miles,
And long ago can be right here,
    right now,
Complete with love and laughter,
Tears and smiles.

Virginia Blanck Moore

Photos courtesy of the Milwaukee Public Museum

The White Frame Church of Old

The fondest of the memories
The years have let me hold
Was built upon a gentle slope . . .
That white frame church of old.

Its steeple pointed far above
As if designed to show
The way to peace and sanctity
Within the doors below.

On Sunday mornings we would come,
A song within our hearts,
To blend our voices in the praise
Of goodness He imparts.

What joy for all who gathered there
For fellowship and praise!
What peace was there in brotherhood,
What heartfelt hymns were raised!

No longer is there worship
In that church upon the hill,
But it lives on within my heart . . .
I know it always will.

Craig E. Sathoff

*Where two or three are gathered together
in my name, there am I in the midst of them.*

Matthew 18:20

Spires

No city can be strange if there but rise
The gleam of steeples in its azure skies;
No road is foreign — gray or amber brown,
Which leads me into any distant town —
If spires lift up beyond to welcome me.
Where churches are, my friends will surely be!

"A haven here, a place for peace and rest!"
These gleaming steeples to my soul attest.
"Come, worship here in sweet tranquillity!
Come, meditate!" the steeples say to me.
No city can be strange if there are spires
To mark the place of peace my soul desires.

Julia Lott

Which Are Better . . .

DOGS
or
CATS?

Cats can run and jump and play . . .
Even frighten mice away!
They'll chase a string or piece of yarn,
Help the farmer in his barn.

Dogs can run and romp and wrestle . . .
Sometimes, even chew a tassle!
They'll watch a house all day or night,
Even help to win a fight!

Cats are good, I must agree!
Dogs are good, that's plain to see!
Now, which one is the very best?
The one that makes you happiest!

Kay Hoffman

Photograph opposite:
Pat Powers

Childhood

Marian L. Moore

Oh, dear little girl with your laughing eyes
A-sparkle like dew when the night is past,
I gaze in their depths blue as summer skies,
And pray joys of childhood shall always last.

With your friendly smile and pig-tailed hair,
At your play through the long golden hours,
You go dancing along as light as air,
The fairest of all among the flowers.

I wish I might always keep you like this,
A heart brimming over with joyous song
And laughter as soft as the spring wind's kiss,
Nothing in life that can ever go wrong.

Then, dear little girl, stay just as you are,
A vision of youth . . . my heart's brightest star.

Photograph opposite:
Ted Laatsch Photo

How Many Worlds the World Is!

Join together
the dots and find
three of the animals
in the poem.

How many worlds the world is!
For every kind of being
There is a special kind of world
According to its seeing.

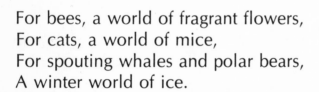

For bees, a world of fragrant flowers,
For cats, a world of mice,
For spouting whales and polar bears,
A winter world of ice.

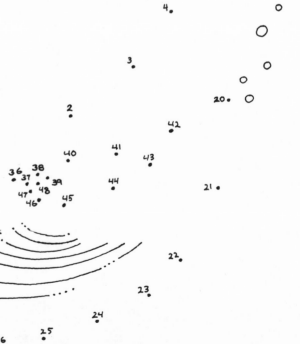

From STORY PARADE, copyright 1954 by
Story Parade, Inc. Reprinted by permission
of Western Publishing Company, Inc.

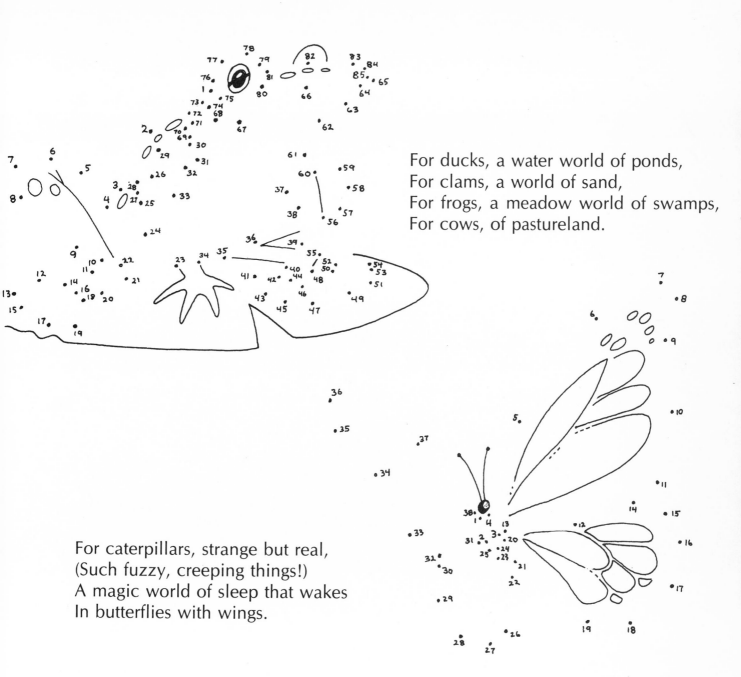

For ducks, a water world of ponds,
For clams, a world of sand,
For frogs, a meadow world of swamps,
For cows, of pastureland.

For caterpillars, strange but real,
(Such fuzzy, creeping things!)
A magic world of sleep that wakes
In butterflies with wings.

A world for everything that lives,
A world for you and me,
Containing all the creature worlds
Of earth and air and sea.

Florence P. Jansson

Beside the Sea

Eleanor Elkins

What shall we look for beside the sea,
On the wide, wet beach where the wind blows free,
Where gulls complain in their ocean home,
As they search for food in the swirling foam.

Come, let us wander among the rocks,
Search for starfish beneath the docks;
Here is a conch shell of delicate pink,
There's a fan of white and a coral link.

That piece of driftwood looks like a horse.
The distant booming shows the force
Of mighty waves as they beat the shore,
Then gather strength to return once more.

Oh, what shall we look for beside the sea?
Big freighters laden with rice and tea
Just in from lands so faraway;
Some will be gone at the break of day.

Trawlers that go to the fishing banks,
Lobster pots marching in serried ranks,
A graceful yacht riding the restless waves,
Seals sporting about near the black sea caves.

Oh, what shall we look for beside the sea,
On that stretch of beach where the wind blows free?
Only a host of exciting things . . .
So, come, let us search, while the ocean sings.

Heritage

Where did you play when you were a child?
Tell me... where were you born?
Did you run on the prairie, free and wild,
And hide in the rows of corn?

Did you open your eyes to a mountaintop?
Did you wiggle your toes in the sand?
Did you play hopscotch in front of a shop?
Or did you live close to the land?

Where were you born and where did you play?
Tell me, and I shall know,
For your past is a part of you still today,
And your youth you will never outgrow.

Eleanor Graham Vance

Children

Children are so many things,

Laughter on a long rope swing,
Ice cream cones and sticky faces,
Boats sailing to faraway places,
A tot in cowboy jeans and shirt,
A ten-year-old in last year's skirt,
Snowsuits and wet wool mittens,
Puppy dogs and fuzzy kittens,
Pretty stones, all kinds of bugs,
Sometimes unexpected hugs,
Birthday parties, lots of toys,
Black, brown, blonde-haired girls and boys,
Stubborn cowlicks, wavy tresses,
Little girls in mommy's dresses,
Questions, answers, many school books,
Happy smiles and worried looks,
An angel at three or an angel at seven,

Children are an earthly bit of heaven.

Ellen G. King

I Saw Beauty

I saw beauty in a vase,
Fragrance, loveliness divine,
Filling up my heart with rapture
That this beauty could be mine.

Spilling beauty in profusion
From a quaint old-fashioned vase,
Common flowers, not rare orchids,
Blooming there in dainty grace.

Some have searched in vain for beauty,
Traveling far to distant place,
But I found it on my table . . .
I saw beauty in a vase.

Edna Greene Hines

The Little Things

It's the little things in life that count,
  The things of every day;
Just the simple things that we can do,
  The kind words we can say.

The little things like a friendly smile
  For those who may be sad,
The clasp of a hand or kindly deed
  To help make someone glad.

A knock on the door of lonely homes,
  Or flowers bright and gay
For someone to whom you might bring cheer
  With just a small bouquet.

Just the little greetings here and there
  On which so much depends,
The little pleasures that all can share,
  The joy of making friends.

Virginia Katherine Oliver

Photograph opposite:
Photo Media Ltd.

Portrait of a Friendship

Faith Baldwin and Gladys Taber

*. . . now and then someone writes a cookbook with a
running commentary, spiced with humor, and gentle with
reminiscence. These I read the way you'd read a novel.*

One such is Gladys Taber's **Stillmeadow Cookbook.** *I can read
that, think myself back to Stillmeadow itself, the old house in
the woods, the hills and the meadows, and the Cape, and
relive our years of friendship.*

Faith Baldwin

In midwinter, Faith Baldwin comes for a visit. We may not have seen each other since fall, but Faith blows in like a leaf (all eighty-five pounds of her), picking up the conversation where we left off when we said good-bye. We talk right on through the day and far into the night, and I am glad no tape recorder is around because we skip from the world situation to the latest Bruce Catton book, from the new styles in clothes (we never like them) to what the children (her three and my one) have been doing.

Faith is a companion for good times but also for difficult ones, for her spirit is as valiant as her tongue is witty. The time the furnace went off in the night and it was ten degrees below zero, Jill and I were in a dither; but Faith appeared for breakfast in her fur coat and said probably someone would fix it in time. When the stove went off, she said sandwiches were fine and cold coffee was good for you. And when we have a flat tire, she comments on what a lovely day it is. Nothing disturbs her inner tranquillity, and yet she is not what most

people think of as a tranquil person: she is volatile and quick, with moods as variable as quicksilver itself.

She is equally at home at an elegant party or sitting in the kitchen eating milk toast. She loves mashed potatoes and gravy, fried tomatoes, salt pork in creamed sauce, and most of the less gourmet foods just as well as lobster soufflé or trout amandine.

When we discuss ourselves, as we do now and then, she says I am too outgoing; I just love everybody, but when I dislike someone it is lethal. I tell her she has a gift for analyzing everyone she sees, but she can be too critical. At that point we generally go back to our jigsaw puzzle and work in silence.

Friendship is a treasure that cannot be overrated. Sometimes as we dash through life, I think, we fail to consider that without the holding of friends (that is the only word for it) we should be in quicksand much of the time. The few people I know who take no pains to be friends are a stern and rock-bound sort and, I notice, seldom

laugh. When I happen to see them, I feel a bridge of distance like the Golden Gate is between my shore and theirs.

With a friendship such as I have with Faith, there is a sharing of the essential self which makes one a better person, I think. We are closely attuned; often I say the first word of a sentence and she completes it, or if we are out with a number of people someone will make a remark and by a flick of an eyelash we tell each other just what we think of that idea.

Yet some people are surprised at this since we are so different, as people keep pointing out, and have been for thirty years. They tell me I am a housewife at heart, a cook, a dog addict, a cat lover, a pushover for babies; whereas she doesn't know how to measure a cup of anything, is never involved with a vacuum cleaner, has no dog or cat, and never acts like an idiot at seeing a baby go by in a carriage. But I think a lifelong friendship is founded, not on two people being alike but in a deeper sense of community spirit. Faith's compassion and inherent sensibility and devotion to large issues and generosity are basic, so why should I care whether she knows how to make a cheese soufflé or cope with burned-out light bulbs?

That old tired saying, "No man is an island," is profoundly true. A sea of differences may stretch between two people, but it is possible to cross it if both are willing.

Gladys Taber

Dough Dolls

a tradition you can bake

Dough art, as ancient as bread making itself, can be a wonderfully relaxing and satisfying hobby, especially during the holiday season. Friends will appreciate a home-baked gift meant to be kept and treasured, not eaten.

Traditional Ecuadorian "Guaguas De Pan" were intricately formed dolls made of bread dough, baked and set out for display on religious occasions. All were beautifully detailed and delicately colored after baking.

The recipe is a simple one. Mix together four cups of flour, one cup of salt, and one and seven-eighths cups of water for seven or eight minutes. Roll a walnut-sized piece of dough into a smooth ball for the head, placing on a non-stick or a waxed-paper-lined cookie sheet. Add a body made from crinkled foil. Shape tubular arms and legs and set in place.

Now roll a piece of dough with a rolling pin into a pie-thin square. Cut articles of clothing from this and attach onto the doll with a few drops of water. Add as many different layers of this dough "clothing" as you wish, making sure to apply a few drops of water between the layers. If you desire to tint a portion of the dough, food colors work well.

Roll a tiny ball for the nose and force a bit of dough through a garlic press for realistic-looking hair. Form the eyes and mouth with a straw or wooden dowel. Now is the time to add patterns to your doll's clothes, such as checks made with a sharp knife, or polka dots added with a straw.

Brush the parts you wish to be browned with canned milk. Now set in the oven for one or two hours at 275°. Remove when hardened and let cool completely before varnishing. Varnish the back as well as the front to repel moisture.

Glue your complete doll onto a plaque made of wood or cardboard covered with contact paper. Wrap it up as a unique gift for a friend, or display one or more on your wall to add a lovely homespun touch to your holiday decor.

Nita Cain

Little deeds of kindness,
Little words of love,
Help to make earth happy,
Like the Heaven above.

Julia Fletcher Carney

Doors

I think a house can never hide
The character of folk inside;
For doors, just hanging in their place,
Like features on an adult's face,
Reveal to all who care to see
The marks of personality.

Some doors are stern with iron or brass,
Some have peepholes of window glass,
And there are paneled ones which plea
Like quiet men for privacy,
While others close their shutters thin
To squint at those who can't see in.

I like a door that opens wide
To share the sounds of life inside . . .
Sounds of boys who hammer nails,
Of girls who practice simple scales,
Sounds of dishes, pots and pans,
Of vacuums and electric fans.

I like a door that speaks to me
Of warmth and hospitality . . .
One that bears a smudge or two
To show that children have pushed through,
And on whose step a friendly cat
Lies curled upon the welcome mat . . .

For they who own a door like this
Dwell where love and warmth exist.

Julia Hurd Strong

Be Delightful, My House

Be strong, my house,
to keep without
the winds that blow too cold,
and keep within the friendliness
that nurtures young and old.

Be bright, my house,
with fires lit
and warmth to spread to all,
and candlelight and lamps aglow
that welcome those who call.

Rejoice, my house,
where happiness
and hope are honeycombed,
for warmth and love and friendship mean
delightful is my home.

Virginia Covey Boswell

I'm Glad That You're

My Neighbor

We share a cheerful greeting
Every time you pass my way;
You lend a helping hand no matter
What the time of day.

We share a cup of coffee and
A bit of humor, too,
And confide our inmost thoughts and dreams
As good friends often do.

You comfort me in sorrow
With a helping hand to lend;
And folks tell me I'm fortunate
To have you for a friend.

I'm glad that you're my neighbor,
And someday I hope to be
The special kind of neighbor
That you have been to me!

Patricia Mongeau

THE CRAZE FOR QUILTS

Wendy Murphy

Blazing Star

Blazing Star

Baby Blocks

*Q*uilting is a craft with a homely history that goes as far back as the Romans and probably even farther back to the ancient Chinese. But it took the Americans to find fun in the doing, thereby creating a folk art that is uniquely our own and uniquely vital today. Sociable busywork for some, creative art for others, sources of income for still others, quilting has been revived and its practitioners can once again be found at their needles from coast to coast.

To put quilting in its simplest terms, ancient craftsmen discovered that two layers of fabric could be made into a warm coverlet if separated by some sort of insulating filler and the whole held together by a few sturdy stitches, called counter points or quilt points. As the craft evolved, these stitches were worked into ever more elaborate linear patterns that became a decorative end in themselves. The first quilted bedcovers produced in America were as close to their English prototypes as memory and a limited supply of imported yard goods could make them. But the high cost and difficulty of obtaining materials led the hard-pressed colonial housewife to improvise, and therein lies the origin of the piecework quilt.

Two centuries before anyone gave a name to it, the thrifty woman of the New World recycled every usable scrap of retired clothing, bedding, and upholstery fabric, sewing them together until she had pieces large enough to cover a bed. On a surface already so busy with color and pattern, she was inclined to make her quilting stitches less showy than English taste demanded. The finished job was called, somewhat apologetically, a Hit-and-Miss or Crazy Quilt.

Eventually, mills began to produce fabrics that were cheap and plentiful on this side of the Atlantic. Presumably many women could go back to doing things the easier way. Just the opposite happened. It's apparent from the great burst of quilt making in the nineteenth century that it was the very difficulty of the task that satisfied, for the make-do crazy quilts of old were joined by still more complicated pieced and patched designs. The chief difference was that the creator was free to *plan* the arrangement of pieces, to cut the fabric to suit the quilt rather than the other way around. The bedcover now became a "canvas" on which a woman could paint with fabric, expressing all her innate sense of color and form.

Her budget and the pattern she chose determined how the quilt would be constructed: pieced quilts, which might consist of several thousand segments, were suited to geometrical designs; the patched or

A "friendship quilt" was made by a group of women as a gift to a neighbor or to an entire family. Often each woman embroidered her name on one of the squares she had sewn as a sign of friendship. Because these quilts were commonly reserved for special use, many that are found today in attic trunks remain in very fine condition.

appliquéd quilt was somewhat more wasteful of material in that the ornamental parts were laid on a background fabric, but with a compensatory gain in design flexibility. Either way the quilt maker usually worked out her motif so that it could be repeated in uniformly sized squares, convenient for carrying about and working, one at a time, in idle moments.

A star, a flower, a wreath, a patriotic symbol and abstract arrangements of circles, triangles and squares were favorite motifs, recast again and again as women traded ideas with one another. Sometimes the name of the pattern stuck — Goose Tracks, Courthouse Steps and Log Cabin seem to have meant

the same thing to the ladies of Maine and Colorado; but often pattern names were changed to suit the commonplaces of the region in which they were used. Typically, the eastern Ship's Wheel became Prairie Star when translated to the frontier; Le Moyne Star, which originally paid homage to an early governor of French Louisiana, was simplified in other parts to Lemon Star. Whimsy and a rugged sort of imagery named such patterns as Puss-in-the-Corner, Drunkard's Path, Hearts and Gizzards, Delectable Mountains, Old Maid's Ramble and Wild Goose Chase.

Once a woman completed all her squares she seamed them together. Then, laying the completed

top on the floor, she traced with chalk or pencil the stitch lines the quilters were to follow. Lastly, she basted top, filler and bottom together.

Only then were the neighbors invited to join her in that happy institution known as the quilting bee, a most descriptive term for the buzzing conviviality that accompanied a session at the quilting frame. In a time when idleness was judged a sin, these cooperative sewing parties were a welcome excuse for getting together. As invitations went most often to those with nimble fingers, it was a wise young woman who made her quilter's reputation early in life and insured her social success.

Continued

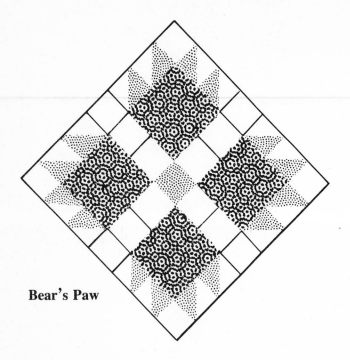

Bear's Paw

Life is like a patchwork quilt,
Little squares of every hue,
Some of silk and calico,
Some of pink and gold and blue.

But each piece will do its part,
Help to make the pattern fine.
When at last the quilt is spread,
Lovely is its whole design.

Georgia Day Sherwood

The party was an all-day affair, starting early in the morning when the ladies set up the frame and "put in" or stretched the basted coverlet over its four sides. Then, taking their places — usually two ladies to a side — they began to stitch their way toward the center. As the work progressed, conversation spilled forth. Harriet Beecher Stowe in her novel *The Minister's Wooing* describes a New England bee circa 1860. "One might have learned in that instructive assembly how best to keep moths out of blankets, how to make fritters of Indian corn undistinguishable from oysters; how to bring up babies by hand; how to reconcile absolute decrees with free will; how to make five yards of cloth answer the purpose of six; and how to put down the Democratic party."

At day's end, the men came to admire the finished work and to collect wives and sisters. Usually they stayed for a festive supper. When the quilt was intended for some special purpose, a bridal quilt for example, the frolicking was

likely to be all the gayer, with singing, dancing and gallant toasts. Young girls traditionally made a number of everyday quilts — perhaps a dozen — in preparation for marriage, so when this, her "best" quilt, was put on the frame, it was tantamount to an engagement announcement. Quilts could also be group gifts, in which many hands produced both the patchwork and the quilting; a "freedom quilt" marked the coming of age of a young man; an "album quilt" was a sort of testimonial to some honored member of the community; a "friendship quilt" might be given to a family that had suffered some reverse. For the bereaved family, there even were "mourning quilts" (black and white only) and "memory quilts" that incorporated scraps of the departed's clothing.

Some time around the 1870's the craft suffered a marked decline. Mass-produced blankets and a greater freedom for women made both the quilt and the quilting bee obsolete in all but the most rural areas. Aunt Indy's Monkey Wrench

and Miss Ida's Churn Dasher were banished to the attic trunk. Today these ladies would be astonished to see their work hanging on museum walls and studied in scholarly journals.

Despite all the recent excitement, it's still not too late for the amateur collector to find old treasures in out-of-the-way places, and new ones in little pockets of America where women supplement their income by making patchworks in the traditional way. But there's nothing mysterious about the technique of quilting and if you can't find the patchwork you want, why not make it. As one Yankee punster put it, quilt making is a great way "to keep the peace and get rid of the scraps."

A good idea any time.

The patchwork pillows shown in the photograph opposite are available in kit form through the Special Selections listed on the order blank. Quilts in photograph courtesy of Mrs. Leila Hentzen Smith. Photo – Ralph Luedtke

The muffled echo of the rooster's crow
Just before the sun rose o'er the hill,
A snapping beam, a sudden thud of snow,
And morning crept across the needled chill
Of wintry night; from valley chimneys rose
White plumes of smoke, inside, bright fires glowed
Through open draughts, while from the kettle's nose
A billowing singing steam cloud flowed.

Winter Memory

The iron griddle soon browned bubbling cakes,
The red checked cloth upon the table spread
Still in my heart an old-time song awakes,
And pictures from a time long since fled.

The old black stove and its rosy embers,
Sweet woodsmoke, a plant upon the sill,
The cozy warmth and peace my heart remembers,
The old clock's steady tick, the lovely thrill
At rainbow lights through icicles reflected,
And warm new milk within an earthen mug . . .
No farther than these walls my thoughts deflected,
Contented as the curled cat on the rug.

Ruth B. Field

WINTER MORNING IN THE COUNTRY
Currier & Ives

THE FARMER'S HOME — WINTER
Currier & Ives

His Friendly Light

How sweet the peace upon the hill . . .
When woodsmoke lingers in the wintry chill;
When my neighbor's lantern with its flickering light
Carves a pathway through the snowdrifts in the night.

How sweet the peace upon the hill . . .
When the fir trees tower statuesque and still,
And even the faintest whisper of a breeze
Dares not to stir or ruffle one of these.

How sweet the peace upon the hill . . .
When the stars look down and see the night fulfilled,
And aught but my neighbor, a deer and a cottontail
Trudge the snowbound slopes and leave their trails.

And what a comfort, what a joy to me
At eventide to gaze at yonder hill and see
His lantern, and then his lamp's flaming wick
In his window glowing, like a beacon o'er the drifts.

As the moonlight bathes all in its silvery glow,
A stillness sweeps across the snow,
And his lamp flickers out,
    and down the rolling slopes I find
Only peace that links his house with mine.

Joy Belle Burgess

The sacrifice of a friend gave the world a beloved masterpiece of art we know as the "Praying Hands." The story behind it? One of love, pathos and unselfish, sacrificial friendship.

The Praying Hands

Along about 1490, two young friends, Albrecht Dürer and Franz Knigstein, were struggling young artists. Since both were very poor, they worked to support themselves while they studied art.

Work took much of their time and advancement was slow. Finally they reached an agreement: they would draw lots, and one of them would work to support both of them while the other would study art. Albrecht won and began to study art while Franz labored to support them both. They agreed that when Albrecht was successful, he would support Franz who would then study art.

Albrecht went off to the cities of Europe to study. As the world now knows, he had not only talent, but genius. When he had attained success, he went back to keep his bargain with Franz. But Albrecht soon discovered the enormous price his friend had paid. For as Franz worked at hard manual labor to support his friend, his fingers had become stiff and twisted. His slender, sensitive hands had been ruined for life. He could no longer execute the delicate brush strokes necessary to fine painting. Though his artistic dreams could never be realized, he was not embittered, but rather, rejoiced in his friend's success.

One day Dürer came upon his friend unexpectedly, and found him kneeling with his gnarled hands intertwined in prayer, quietly praying for the success of his friend although he himself could no longer be an artist. Albrecht Dürer, the great genius, hurriedly sketched the folded hands of his faithful friend and later completed a truly great masterpiece known as the *Praying Hands*.

Today, art galleries everywhere feature Albrecht Dürer's works. But of them all, none holds the place in the hearts of people that *Praying Hands* does. It tells an eloquent story of love, sacrifice, labor and gratitude. And it has reminded multitudes the world around of how they also may find comfort, courage and strength.

J. Palmer Muntz

Navajo Child

What are you dreaming of, Navajo child,
There in your desert, lonely and wild!
Do the soft, sighing winds whisper secrets to you?
Do the white clouds make pictures in skies clean and blue?

Do you hear the jay calling from wind-sheltered bower?
Do you savor the perfume of white cactus flower?
Are you happy to look on the wide, painted land . . .
Are you awed by the work of the Great Father's hand?

Your eager brown hands mold the future, unseen;
Your heart holds the hope of your people, serene.
But your dark, haunting eyes by your dreaming beguiled . . .
What do they see, little Navajo child?

Ruth K. Hall

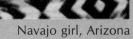

Never lose an opportunity
of seeing anything that is
beautiful; for beauty is
God's handwriting . . . a
wayside sacrament . . .

Navajo mother and child, Arizona

Navajo girl, Arizona

Welcome it in every fair
face, in every fair sky, in
every fair flower, and
thank God for it as a cup of
blessing.

Ralph Waldo Emerson

*Overleaf: Grand Canyon,
Arizona. Photo - Alpha*

Walk on a rainbow trail, walk on a trail of song,
and all about you will be beauty. There is a way
out of every dark mist, over a rainbow trail.

Navajo Song

The Path
of the
Padres

Long, long ago, the padres
  With weary feet, and slow,
Marked out this earliest highway
  And showed the way to go
From mission unto mission
  Through all the golden land,
Bright with the glow of poppies
  That bloomed on every hand.

Across a sage-grown upland
  Once, on a summer day,
I found an old path, winding
  Its long-forgotten way,
Half hidden by tall grasses
  That surged up from the vale
And nodded heads of silver
  Along the lonely trail.

The padres long are sleeping
  At peace beneath the sod,
And a more stately highway
  Outlines the way they trod;
But ah — across the uplands
  And over the brown hill,
The little path, forgotten,
  Winds on in beauty still.

Edith D. Osborne

Photograph opposite: Mission San Xavier del Bac, near Tucson, Arizona. This beautiful church was built by Franciscans between 1783 and 1797 and represents a graceful blending of Moorish Byzantine and late Mexican Renaissance architectures. Known as the ''White Dove of the Desert,'' it is the third church at Bac, an Indian settlement first visited by a Jesuit missionary, Father Eusebio Francisco Kino, in 1692. Photo — Robert F. Campbell

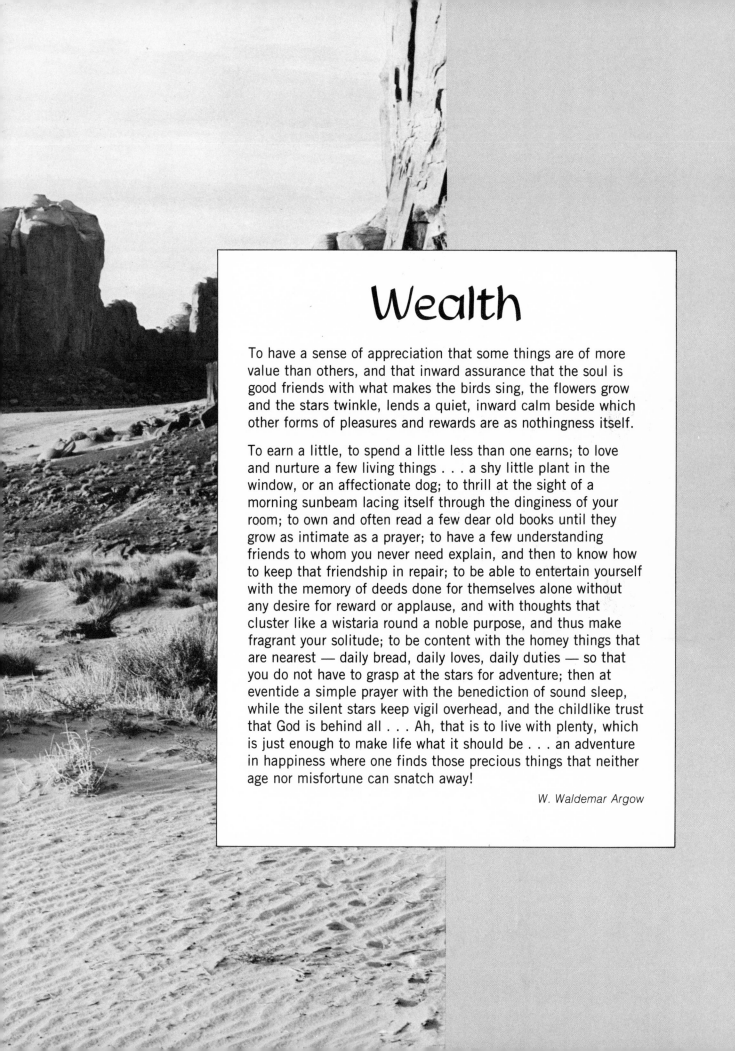

Wealth

To have a sense of appreciation that some things are of more value than others, and that inward assurance that the soul is good friends with what makes the birds sing, the flowers grow and the stars twinkle, lends a quiet, inward calm beside which other forms of pleasures and rewards are as nothingness itself.

To earn a little, to spend a little less than one earns; to love and nurture a few living things . . . a shy little plant in the window, or an affectionate dog; to thrill at the sight of a morning sunbeam lacing itself through the dinginess of your room; to own and often read a few dear old books until they grow as intimate as a prayer; to have a few understanding friends to whom you never need explain, and then to know how to keep that friendship in repair; to be able to entertain yourself with the memory of deeds done for themselves alone without any desire for reward or applause, and with thoughts that cluster like a wistaria round a noble purpose, and thus make fragrant your solitude; to be content with the homey things that are nearest — daily bread, daily loves, daily duties — so that you do not have to grasp at the stars for adventure; then at eventide a simple prayer with the benediction of sound sleep, while the silent stars keep vigil overhead, and the childlike trust that God is behind all . . . Ah, that is to live with plenty, which is just enough to make life what it should be . . . an adventure in happiness where one finds those precious things that neither age nor misfortune can snatch away!

W. Waldemar Argow

Friends

Friends are keys to unlock the heart,
To find the joys love can impart,
To discover the treasures rare,
To discern what it means to share.

Some keys are worn, like burnished gold . . .
These are old friends who've passed time's test;
They will accept you, weak or strong,
But they demand of you your best.
They lift you up when spirits sag,
Share the laughter, comfort the tears;
They understand the inmost thoughts,
Give faith for doubts, courage for fears.

Some keys are shining like silver . . .
These are new friends you're getting to know,
And you'll walk along together
As you weather life's ebb and flow;
Some days will be bright with rapture,
Others dark with impending storm,
But friendship welcomes each new day
As cares grow light and hearts grow warm.

It takes both kinds of keys in life:
Both kinds of friends, both tried and true,
One kindles memories of the past,
One holds the torch to blaze trails new.
Both lead one onward and upward
With a smile, a touch or a prayer,
With patience and understanding,
With concern that is loving care.

So "make new friends, but keep the old,
One is silver, the other gold" . . .
Through every day each plays a part,
Each a key to unlock the heart.

Erma Stull Grove

Statement of ownership, management and circulation required by Act of Congress of August 24, 1912, as amended by the Acts of March 3, 1933, and July 2, 1946, and June 11, 1960 (74 Stat. 208), and October 23, 1962 (Section 4369, Title 30. United States Code), and August 12, 1970 (Section 3685, Title 39. United States Code) of IDEALS, published bimonthly at Milwaukee, Wisconsin for September 1974. Editor, Maryjane Hooper Tonn; Managing Editor, Lorraine Obst; Owner, Ideals Publishing Corp., 11315 Watertown Plank Road, Milwaukee, Wisconsin 53226. Stockholders owning or holding one percent or more of total amount of stock: The Ideals Corporation, 11315 Watertown Plank Road, Milwaukee, Wisconsin, 53226. The known bondholders, mortgagees, and other security holders owning or holding one percent or more of total amount of bonds, mortgages or other securities are: None. Average no. copies each issue preceding 12 months: Total no. copies printed (net press run) 231,976. Paid circulation 78,932, other sales, 148,094. Free distribution 400, Total no. of copies distributed 227,426. Single issue nearest to filing date: Total no. of copies printed (net press run) 188,769. Paid circulation 33,070, other sales 145,118. Free distribution 400. Total no. of copies distributed 178,588. I certify that the statements made by me are correct and complete. Theodore E. Saleske, Vice President-Finance

Photograph opposite
YUCCAS AT SUNSET
near Oracle, Arizona
Photo – Josef Muench

Gene Ahrens

The Fellowship of Friends

Take time for all things...
The day is too long
Without joy and laughter,
Without a song.

Take time for all things...
Share the gift of work and play;
Weave the golden thread of love
Into the fabric of each day.

Take time for all things...
Give thanks to Him who sends
The benediction of His love
And the fellowship of friends.

Clara Smith Reber

In our next issue, **EASTER IDEALS 1975,** we are including these features...

THE EASTER STORY ... the dramatic account of the Passion Week with beautiful color illustrations

WHY EGGS IN YOUR EASTER ... the story behind the custom of decorating eggs

THE ISLE OF EMERALD ... a view of Ireland and its Easter customs

THE TALE OF PETER RABBIT ... Beatrix Potter's perennial favorite for young folks

FOR THE BEAUTY OF THE EARTH... the origin of a best-loved hymn

PLUS ... inspiring prose and poetry of Easter and springtime as written by your favorite IDEALS authors.

Acknowledgments: *". . . NOW AND THEN SOMEONE WRITES . . ." by Faith Baldwin. From EVENING STAR by Faith Baldwin. Copyright © 1964 by Faith Baldwin Cuthrell. Reprinted by permission of Holt, Rinehart and Winston, Inc. FRIENDS by Erma Stull Grove. From THE FOOTPRINT OF GOD by Erma Stull Grove. Copyright © 1969 by Erma Stull Grove. Published by Dorrance & Company. WILLOW PATTERN by Amanda Benjamin Hall. Originally published in GOURMET, January 1973. Used with permission. "I REMEMBER THE MORNING . . ." by Helen Keller. From THE STORY OF MY LIFE by Helen Keller. Used through courtesy of Doubleday & Company, Inc. THE PRAYING HANDS by J. Palmer Muntz. From THE GOLD STAR FAMILY ALBUM, 1968. Used by permission of the author. DOORS by Julia Hurd Strong. From POSTLUDE TO MENDELSSOHN, Copyright © 1964 by Julia Hurd Strong. HERITAGE by Eleanor Graham Vance. Copyright by Eleanor Graham Vance. Used by permission of the author. Our sincere thanks to the following authors whose addresses we were unable to locate for material in this book: Edward Verrall Lucas for FRIENDS, L. M. Montgomery for I WISH YOU, Edith D. Osborne for THE PATH OF THE PADRES.*

Our special thanks to Nancy McCauley of Oak Ridge, Tennessee, for her original needlepoint design on the front and back covers.

Additional photo credits: *Inside covers by Gene Ahrens.*

My Personal Order

YOUR NAME _____ Please print clearly

ADDRESS _____

CITY _____ (   ) _____

STATE _____ *ZIP CODE _____

MY IDEALS SUBSCRIPTION BLANK

CHECK ✓	SUBSCRIPTIONS WILL BEGIN WITH ISSUE MARKED	✓ CHECK STARTING IDEALS ISSUE
	*4 VOL. SUBSCRIPTION (4 consecutive issues) @ $6.00 BEGIN ☐FRIENDSHIP ☐EASTER ☐OLD FASHIONED IDEALS	
	*1 YEAR SUBSCRIPTION (6 consecutive issues) @ $8.50 BEGIN ☐FRIENDSHIP ☐EASTER ☐OLD FASHIONED IDEALS	
➤	SPECIAL—First one yr. subscription $8.50 1-4 additional gift subscriptions $7.50 or a total of 5 or more additional gift subscriptions $7.00	
	*2 YEAR SUBSCRIPTION (12 consecutive issues) @ $16.00 BEGIN ☐FRIENDSHIP ☐EASTER ☐OLD FASHIONED IDEALS	
	SPECIAL—FREE WITH EACH 2 YR. SUBSCRIPTION A GREETINGS BOOKLET PACK (5 booklets all occasion)	
	PAY AS YOU READ (1 copy each issue with invoice for $1.75) BEGIN ☐FRIENDSHIP ☐EASTER ☐OLD FASHIONED IDEALS	

*Your Subscription will begin with FRIENDSHIP unless otherwise indicated.

BEAUTIFUL IDEALS ISSUES 8½ x 11

QUANTITY	TITLE	PRICE	QUANTITY	TITLE	PRICE
	FRIENDSHIP	$2.25		COUNTRY ROADS	$1.95
	EASTER IDEALS (NEW)	$2.25		SUNNY DAYS	$1.95
	FAMILY	$1.95		IDEALS BINDER (Holds 6 Issues)	$4.00

LOVELY HARD BOUND BOOKS 8½ x 11 . . . * 11 x 8½

QUANTITY	TITLE	PRICE	QUANTITY	TITLE	PRICE
	LOVE IS . . . OH SO MANY THINGS*	$5.00		SCRAPBOOK FAVORITES	$2.95
	BECAUSE YOU ARE MY FRIEND*	$5.00		THOUGHTS FOR ALL SEASONS	$2.95
	MASTERPIECES OF RELIGIOUS ART	$3.50		JUST BETWEEN FRIENDS	$2.95
	HOW GREAT THOU ART (NEW)	$3.50		I WILL LIFT UP MINE EYES	$2.95
	WOMEN IN AMERICA (NEW)	$3.50		AMERICA CELEBRATES (A)	$2.50
	THE JOYS OF EASTER (NEW)	$3.50		YOU'RE A GRAND OLD FLAG (Y)	$2.50
	MOTHERS ARE VERY SPECIAL (NEW)	$3.50		MOMENTS OF PRAYER	$2.50
	PASSING SCENE	$3.50		I REMEMBER, DO YOU?	$2.50
	WOODLAND PORTRAITS	$3.50		SPECIAL—SET (AY) (2 Books—Save 2.50)	$2.50
	IT'S GOOD TO REMEMBER	$3.00			
	A BOOK OF MEMORIES	$2.95			

HARD BOUND GIFT BOOKS 5⅜ x 7½

QUANTITY	TITLE	PRICE	QUANTITY	TITLE	PRICE
	PRAYERS FOR DAILY LIVING (NEW)	$2.00		FOR MOTHER WITH LOVE	$2.00
	THOUGHTS TO LIVE BY	$2.00		MESSAGES OF FAITH	$2.00
	I LOVE YOU BECAUSE	$2.00		BIRTHDAYS ARE SPECIAL	$2.00

COOK BOOKS BY IDEALS 8½ x 11

QUANTITY	TITLE	PRICE	QUANTITY	TITLE	PRICE
	GOURMET ON THE GO (NEW)	$1.75		THE IDEALS FAMILY DESSERT COOK BOOK	$1.75
	IDEALS OUTDOOR COOK BOOK (NEW)	$1.75		THE IDEALS WHOLE GRAIN COOK BOOK	$1.75
	THE IDEALS ALL HOLIDAY COOK BOOK	$1.75		THE IDEALS FAMILY COOK BOOK VOL II	$1.50
	THE IDEALS FAMILY GARDEN COOK BOOK	$1.75		THE IDEALS FAMILY COOK BOOK	$1.50

SPECIAL CHILDREN'S BOOKS 8½ x 11 SOFT COVER

QUANTITY	TITLE	PRICE	QUANTITY	TITLE	PRICE
	STORY BOOK FAVORITES (HARD BOUND)	$3.00		FOR LITTLE SLEEPY HEADS	$1.00
	EASTER STORIES FOR CHILDREN (NEW)	$1.25		OLD KING COLE	$1.00
	BUNNY TALES	$1.00		ZIGGY, WHAT ANIMALS SAY	$1.00

DISTINCTIVE GREETING BOOKLETS 5⅜ x 7¼ SAVE $1.00. ORDER 10 THEN DEDUCT $1.00 FROM TOTAL

QUANTITY	TITLE	PRICE	QUANTITY	TITLE	PRICE
	TO MY VALENTINE (NEW)	75¢		QUIET MOMENTS	75¢
	ON VALENTINE'S DAY	60¢		SENDING SUNSHINE YOUR WAY	60¢
	A JOYFUL EASTER (NEW)	75¢		THINKING OF YOU ESPECIALLY TODAY	60¢
	REMEMBERING MOTHER WITH LOVE (NEW)	75¢		BECAUSE YOU'RE YOU	60¢
	FOR DAD (NEW)	75¢		HOPE IT'S A HAPPY DAY	60¢
	ON FATHER'S DAY	60¢		TOUCH OF FRIENDSHIP	60¢
	TO THE GRADUATE (NEW)	75¢		WORDS OF INSPIRATION	60¢
	IT'S ALWAYS FUN TO WISH YOU A HAPPY BIRTHDAY (NEW)	75¢		IN THE KITCHEN	60¢
	REMEMBERING YOUR BIRTHDAY	75¢		TELL ME A STORY (CHILDREN'S)	60¢
	HAPPY BIRTHDAY TO YOU	60¢		TO WISH YOU A HAPPY ANNIVERSARY	60¢
	IT'S TIME TO SAY HAPPY BIRTHDAY	60¢		BEST WISHES FOR YOUR ANNIVERSARY	60¢
	HAPPY BIRTHDAY (CHILDREN'S)	60¢		A NEW BABY . . . WHAT WONDERFUL NEWS	60¢
	BLOW OUT THE CANDLES (CHILDREN'S)	60¢		YOUR NEW BABY . . . CONGRATULATIONS	60¢
	MAY ALL YOUR DREAMS COME TRUE	75¢		PLEASE GET WELL	75¢
	ON YOUR WEDDING DAY	75¢		HOPE YOU'RE FEELING BETTER	75¢
	FROM THIS DAY FORWARD	60¢		GET WELL WISHES	60¢
	HOW DO I LOVE THEE (BROWNING)	75¢		IN SYMPATHY	60¢
	YOU HAVE TO BELIEVE	75¢			
	THANK YOU—YOU DO THE NICEST THINGS	75¢			

STATIONERY AND 1975 CALENDAR

QUANTITY	TITLE	PRICE
	SCENE & STRIPES PORTFOLIO OF STATIONERY	$1.25
	IDEALS 1975 MEMORY RECIPE CALENDAR	$2.50

☐ If you wish to receive our Ideals catalog, check here. Enter friends' names under gift area on the back and indicate send catalog.

 ENTER SPECIAL SELECTIONS & GIFT SUBSCRIPTIONS ON REVERSE SIDE ⬅

SPECIAL SELECTIONS

QUANTITY	DESCRIPTION	PRICE
	LIVING BIBLE	$10.95
	CHILDREN'S LIVING BIBLE	$6.45
➤	SPECIAL—BOTH FOR (SAVINGS OF $2.40)	$15.00
	NEW HEIRLOOM BIBLE	
	☐ CATHOLIC ☐ PROTESTANT	$16.95
	PICNIC TOTE BAG	$16.95
	RECORDS	
	DR. FUN'S FUNHOUSE (CHILDREN'S)	$10.98
	LOVE ALBUM—RAY CONNIFF	$12.95
	EASTER ORNAMENT KITS	
	ROSE GARDEN #6148	$3.00
	SECRETS #6149	$3.00
	BRIDE #13304	$3.50
➤	SPECIAL—ANY 3 ORN. KITS FOR	$8.50
	PATCH WORK PILLOW KIT	
	☐ BROWN ☐ RED	$8.50

QUANTITY	DESCRIPTION	PRICE
	MINIATURE OIL LAMPS (WITH OIL) (NO ADDITIONAL POSTAGE)	
	DR. ELY PARSON'S MIRACLE OIL LAMP	$3.95
	THE MILKMAID MINIATURE	$3.95
➤	COUNTY FAIR TWIN SET (BOTH ABOVE)	$6.95
	"HAVING A WONDERFUL TIME" GIFT LAMP	$3.95
	"WISH YOU WERE HERE" GIFT LAMP	$3.95
	"GOOD MORNING, SUNSHINE" GIFT LAMP	$3.95
➤	DOUBLE "HEART WARMERS" (ANY TWO ABOVE)	$6.95

12 TO A BOX NOTES BY IDEALS 4 x 5 @ $1.25

SPECIAL—CHOOSE ANY 4 BOXED NOTES—DEDUCT $.50

BOX 22	$1.25	BOX 26	$1.25
BOX 23	$1.25	BOX 27	$1.25
BOX 24	$1.25	BOX 28	$1.25
BOX 25	$1.25		

OTHER BOXED SET CHOICES INDICATE SET NOS. BELOW

FOLD HERE FIRST

* FOREIGN POSTAGE ONLY

Four Volume Subscription	Add $ .60
One Year Subscription	Add $1.00
Two Year Subscription	Add $2.00
IDEALS Binder	Add $ .50
For all other Single IDEALS PUBLICATIONS	Add $ .50

Wisconsin Residents Please Note:
You must Add 4% sales tax on all products sent to Wisconsin addresses, except bimonthly IDEALS issues and subscriptions to IDEALS bimonthly issues.

68

FOR OFFICE USE ONLY

ENTRD			Type	AMT.
REMTC			IDEALS	
K	Mo	C	Subs	
Checked for Accuracy			Binder	
			Prints	
OVER PAY			Postage	
			Allied Prod	
			P.A.Y.R.	
			NOTES	
			TAX	

FOLD HERE FIRST

THANK YOU!

FOLD SIDE FLAPS FIRST — THEN FOLD HERE

ideals **PUBLISHING CORP.**
11315 WATERTOWN PLANK RD.
MILWAUKEE, WISCONSIN 53201

from _____
_____
ZIP CODE (____)

FOLD SIDE FLAPS FIRST!
When properly sealed with the above gummed flap this envelope and its contents will travel safely through the mail.

IDENTIFY AS A
GIFT FROM_____

TO_____

ADDRESS_____

CITY_____STATE_____ZIP CODE (____)

MAIL DATE & OCCASION_____

QUANTITY	TITLE		PRICE
	*4 Vol. Subscription (4 issues)	@	$6.00
	*1 Yr. Subscription (6 issues)	@	$8.50
	*2 Yr. Subscription (12 issues)	@	$16.00
	LIST OTHER GIFT SELECTIONS BELOW		
	SEND CATALOG ☐		

IDENTIFY AS A
GIFT FROM_____

TO_____

ADDRESS_____

CITY_____STATE_____ZIP CODE (____)

MAIL DATE & OCCASION_____

QUANTITY	TITLE		PRICE
	*4 Vol. Subscription (4 issues)	@	$6.00
	*1 Yr. Subscription (6 issues)	@	$8.50
	*2 Yr. Subscription (12 issues)	@	$16.00
	LIST OTHER GIFT SELECTIONS BELOW		
	SEND CATALOG ☐		

*Gift subscriptions will begin with FRIENDSHIP unless otherwise indicated. Begin with_____